Half-Blood Poems

Inspired by the Stories of
J. K. Rowling

by

Christine Lowther

This book was produced through a printing facility with Chain-of-Custody certification from three leading environmental organizations:

The Sustainable Forestry Initiative® (SFI®)
The Programme for the Endorsement of Forestry Certification (PEFC™)
The Forest Stewardship Council® (FSC™)

Chain of custody (CoC) is an accounting system that tracks wood fiber through the different stages of production: from the forest, to the mill, to the paper, to the printer and ultimately to the finished book. For publishers, and ultimately consumers, CoC ensures the integrity of the paper supply chain and that the paper used in printed books are from responsibly managed forests. Only 10% of the world's forests are certified to any standard and certification promotes responsible forestry globally.

About SFI:
The Sustainable Forestry Initiative® (SFI®) program is an independent, non-profit, organization with a science-based, internationally recognized forest management standard for North America. The SFI program is based on the premise that responsible environmental behavior and sound business decisions can coexist to the benefit of communities, customers and the environment, today and for future generations. Learn more at www.sfiprogram.org

About PEFC:
The Programme for the Endorsement of Forest Certification (PEFC™) is an international non-profit, non-governmental organization dedicated to promoting Sustainable Forest Management (SFM) through independent third-party certification. www.pefc.org

About FSC:
FSC is an independent, non-governmental, not-for-profit organization established to promote the responsible management of the world's forests. Established in 1993 as a response to concerns over global deforestation, FSC is widely regarded as one of the most important initiatives of the last decade to promote responsible forest management worldwide. FSC provides internationally recognized standard-setting, trademark assurance and accreditation services to companies, organizations, and communities interested in responsible forestry. The FSC label provides a credible link between responsible production and consumption of forest products, enabling consumers and businesses to make purchasing decisions that benefit people and the environment as well as providing ongoing business value. FSC is nationally represented in more than 50 countries around the world. www.fsc.org

PRAISE FOR OTHER BOOKS BY CHRISTINE LOWTHER

"Her poems come from the edges of polite society,
of the ocean storm, where unexpected things happen,
where changes occur..."
—**Ursula Vaira**
Prize-winning Poet and Publisher (Leaf Press)

"Lowther's first book, *New Power*, is an
astonishing collection of heartbreaking force."
—**George Elliott Clarke**
Canadian Poet and Playwright

"She has a genius for loci,
the tutelary deity or the pervading spirit of a place."
—**Anne Burke**
Chair, Feminist Caucus, League of Canadian Poets

Half-Blood Poems: Inspired by the Stories of J. K. Rowling
Copyright © 2011 Christine Lowther

Published by Zossima Press
Hamden, CT

10-9-8-7-6-5-4-3-2-1

Zossima
Press

ISBN-13 978-1-935688-04-4

"The books wouldn't be what they are if she hadn't died. I mean, her death is on virtually every other page ... At least half of Harry's journey is a journey to deal with death: in its many forms, what it does to the living, what it means to die, what survives death — it's there in every single volume. ... [T]he books are what they are because she died..."

J. K. Rowling (Oprah Winfrey interview)

CONTENTS

ABOUT THE POEMS

In Canada, where I live, poetry is taken *very* seriously. How does a poet gain and maintain credibility if the words *Star Trek* appear, or vampires (groan) are mentioned? Or – worst of all – *Harry Potter* references are referenced? While writing a book of nature poetry, popular culture kept popping up in my drafts. Luckily, my publisher didn't mind a dementor appearing out of nowhere in a poem about depression, or a spell settling into place in a poem about lightning, and as for a poem about my scar burning, who was to know it was Potter-inspired except the wizard-aware?

These references, as infrequent as they were, seemed irrepressible. One day long after that book came out, I was remembering (for the umpteenth time) the scene in the film version of *Azkaban* when Harry rides Buckbeak over the lake. He lets go of the Hippogriff's neck and sits up, hooting with joy as the wind blows back his hair, revealing his forehead scar. Something of deep personal significance stirred there … suddenly I was reaching for pen and paper. The result was my first fully pop-culture-inspired poem, and my first wholly Potter poem, if you will.

What release and relief it would be, I thought, to be given free rein with these ideas! Instead of having them pop up here and there as references, to allow my muse to be awash in them, revel in unashamed fandom, no longer having to divide my two loves of creative expression (art) and guilty geekdom. I would search for a Potterphile publisher … outside of Canada! And, as you can clearly see, I found one.

The original plan was to write seven poems for each novel/section, but the more I wrote, the more there was to write. The novels are rich and varied, nearly endless in ideas, humor, emotion, relationship, reflection, morality, spiritual struggle, alchemy, and symbolism. The movies are visually beautiful with many moments that can trigger expression, and music that stays with fans for a long time. The poems, to borrow a cliché, almost wrote themselves.

NOTES TO THE POEMS:

Forbidden Forest: Fangorn was an ancient forest in *The Lord of the Rings*.

Scar: This poem was previously published in *My Nature* (Leaf Press). *Carrie* was a horror flick made in the 1970s.

Unspoken Thoughts: Who decides which individuals may have need of the elixir and what it may be used for? Or is there a law in the wizarding world that only alchemists who succeed in making the stone may use it as they see fit? If no law, then Flamel and his wife were being exclusive. How could Dumbledore condone this? He tells Harry that "humans do have a knack of choosing precisely those things that are worst for them." Were the Flamels not happy? Would anyone choose to stay unhappy for over 600 years?

   Did Ms. Rowling make the Hogwarts Headmaster "partners" with Flamel to show how close Dumbledore could get to this particular temptation without using it himself? After all, if Dumbledore were to drink of the elixir and become immortal, it would only mean having to live that much longer without ever seeing his family and begging their forgiveness after death. The other thing provided by the stone, unlimited wealth, equally could have no fascination for such a man as Albus.

For Our Wide-Armed Mothers: Xenophilius Lovegood, a doting father, also spread his arms for his daughter, blockading our heroic trio as they tried to walk out his front door.

Trauma Remedy for Travelers was previously published in *My Nature* (Leaf Press).

Feeling Pensive? and *The Doe*: A 'found poem' is prose taken as it was found within a text and laid out poetically, i.e. hugging the left margin. Another example can be found in Kate Braid's book *To This Cedar Fountain*: the poem "Green Sea" is realigned prose of Emily Carr, found in *Hundreds and Thousands*. We can clearly see and hear how poetic Rowling's prose is here.

The Untamed Fleeing up Trees was previously published in *My Nature* (Leaf Press).

Light and Dark: "Sometimes there is honor in revenge" is a line I have borrowed from Elijah on *The Vampire Diaries* television show.

Long Game Ended, Time to Leave the Air: The poem's title comes from *Deathly Hallows* itself.

ABOUT THE POET

A half-blood is a wizard or witch with one magical parent and one muggle parent. This book is titled *Half-Blood* because of a notable difference between Harry and me. Unlike Harry's mother, Lily, who died at the hands of Voldemort, it was my own father who murdered my mother. He was an unsuccessful poet, a wanna-be poet, if you will. A squib. On the other hand, my mother, Pat Lowther, at the time of her death, was a gifted and successful poet who had shared readings with Margaret Atwood.

But in other ways my life has been eerily like that of "the boy who lived." Here are some of what I call my Searing Similarities to Harry Potter:

1. I lost my parents to murder as a child.
2. I subsequently acquired a scar on my forehead.
3. I was taken in by relatives and often told to be more grateful.
4. I was happier and more at home while in school (eventually).
5. I wasn't crazy about summer break.
6. Harry "has no memory of his parents, only a sense of who they were" (David Jones, *Hog's Head Conversations, p. 194*). Me too.
7. I had a boyfriend whose mother was to me what Molly is to Harry.
8. The way Remus Lupin speaks of Lily in the film version of *Prisoner of Azkaban* is exactly how people still speak of my own mother: uncommonly kind, remarkably gifted etc.
9. I learned from those outside the family of my resemblance to her: the color of my eyes.
10. Hagrid, no relation, gave Harry a precious photo-album of his parents. It was a non-relation who presented my sister and I with the only color photograph of my mother.
11. Lily was a *poetic witch* (think of the lily petal that transformed into a "wee fish", a gift for Professor Slughorn in the film version of *Half-Blood Prince*); my mum was a *magical poet*.
12. We even have an arboreal commonality. The Whomping

Willow was, according to Severus Snape, an "old and valuable tree" – valuable, that is, as it was: alive. It was also dangerous, yet, when damaged, Hogwarts professors went to the trouble of bandaging it and putting several of its branches in slings.

In my small town lives a massive, 800-year-old cedar tree. Local schoolteachers value this tree; when it was threatened by a development of condominiums, a day of photographs and publicity was organized, and several teachers brought their classes to pose in many colors of raingear around the massive trunk. (It rains a lot in my town … like at Hogwarts.) This cedar was also considered dangerous; the developer was afraid it would fall upon his condominiums. After a handful of us blocked a remarkably large chainsaw, two young men set up camp high in its crown and lived there for thirty-five days, while the rest of us raised money to … put the sentinel in a sling, so to speak (guy wires and girdle). To this day the Eik cedar still stands over those condos, buttressed by steel.

J. K. Rowling has said that she enjoyed C.S. Lewis's Narnia series as a child. It is no exaggeration to say that those books helped me survive my childhood. As for Rowling's novels, they have added greatly to a meaningful and healing adulthood. For this, and for their endless inspiration, I am deeply grateful.

To email me, please write to raggy@island.net and visit my blog at: http://christinelowther.blogspot.com. I would love to hear from you.

I

STONES OF SORCERY

LIFE BEFORE EMAIL

When I was a teen mail came
through a slot in the front door,
the waiting, something to savour.
Never plain letters in white envelopes,
nor fearful howlers smoking at the seams,
these were packages, creatively adorned:
the circled A, the mohawked profile.
Inside, handwriting sprawled over the back
of two or three posters of recent gigs;
political pamphlets, animal rights leaflets;
fliers for upcoming shows;
a 'zine or two. From England: *Direct Action*,
Hunt Saboteurs Association.
From Vancouver: *Smarten Up!*,
Terminally Stupid. From the States:
Maximum RocknRoll.
I got more post than any of the adults
in the house. And re-used every stamp,
because punk rockers
soaped their stamps to save money—
licked a finger, rubbed off the ink
like magic.
Some days delivery fountained
like the blizzard flurrying
from Vernon Dursley's fireplace.
Then came the snatching, catching,
unsealing,
and, always,
the astounding good news.

INITIATION

The music, playing *us*, revealed
a place we had hungered for
without fully knowing it.
First glimpse of Diagon was like
walking into Narnia
but with head held high
rather than hiding and sneaking—
better! because it was summer
and there was shopping,
there were owls and bats,
there was magic upon magic,
and we ourselves were hungered for.
With money enough at Gringott's,
here was new beginning: life as if we belonged,
the diagonal rite of passage and right-of-way,
the ultimate alternative subculture.
Merely an appetizer!
We were about to travel further in
to that world, find ourselves
changed with each moving staircase.

CHRISTINE LOWTHER

3

WANDLORE

Wandlore, but not here,
not really, just the word
itself is poetic.
Wandlore 101 from Ollivander,
his face too close to mine.
Before school commences,
I am learning
in the dust and silence
what is terribly important:
that I have my mother's eyes
and our enemy's twin core.

ON THE EXPRESS

Not only am I making a new friend
he's my first friend,
my only friend.
Comes from an entire family
of wizards, I'd be stymied
if he weren't so unassuming,
so *normal*. Even his rat
is as scruffy as my hand-me-down
socks, and what's with all these
magical sweets, these
chocolate frog cards?
Scrumptious, fascinating,
I can't get enough,
and this chap, despite
living all his life with them,
evidently can't either.

SEEKER AND SNITCH

They call me The Seeker
I've been searching low and high
I won't get to get what I'm after
Till the day I die
—The Who

What is this glinting gold
what are these whirring wings
this tiny ball that keeps its memories
of lips and fleshly things?
Is every snitch made to open
a holder of truths so deep
belonging now to its hunter
not only to catch, but to keep?
What is the point of a quaffle
and goalposts when a ball so bright
ends the game,
settles the match,
stops the fight?

FORBIDDEN FOREST

...the forest in the grounds is forbidden...

...it's into the forest you're going
and I'm much mistaken
if you'll all come out in one piece.

Gee, why would a forest be so dangerous?
Let's think. To construct a trail in the old days
we hiked in with our hand-tools, toiled
with respect, minimized damage,
were sensitive to root systems.
Now the machines have moved in
cut their swath, cast kinks
of intestine and bowel,
spewed tree sap and bush blood.
Our feet keep to the centre of the new path
and suffer the truth: we tread
through someone's remains,
stand in their guts,
tempt Devil's Snare.
Not the way I'd beg welcome
from Fangorn,
from any forest, dark or light.
I keep expecting to spot
that mercurious shine
of silver-blue unicorn blood.
Sometimes slow and careful

are the best way, not careless
like the troll with his club;
we have not his excuse.
I squat in the mud
waiting hopelessly for a hero
to undo the mess, for Firenze,
Magorian, Ronan
or even Bane to put it right.
Instead I emerge in one piece
leaving the forest in shards,
not yet slain, pure, defenseless,
a cursed half of what it was.
Who would choose such a crime?

CHRISTINE LOWTHER

CLOAK-AND-MIRROR

All of my life has been
like the constrictor in the zoo
minus a concerned audience
and now this: unhindered,
unimagined freedom
which is my birthright!
Admiring and caressing it,
undecided on whether to share,
show it off or keep it secret
I will spread it across my bed,
hang it on my wall in pride of place,
hold it against the window
to watch the beauty it makes of daylight.
But my dearest desire is
to use it well.

My first unrestricted access
is to the library's restricted section:
something useful, we had thought. Not!
Ideas race: eavesdropping, staffroom,
the other common rooms,
girls' dorms and bathrooms,
the prefects' rooms,
the kitchens. For a moment,
I am unfocussed.
Then I find the mirror.

Half joy, half terrible sadness,
my hunger for what I see here
reflects more: starvation,
this heart famished for them.
The glass, impervious to these hands
locks heart-threads in place.
The cloak can only be used
for one thing, now: getting me
to Erised every night.

When the headmaster
absconds with the mirror
I wrap invisibility
around my cold body
burrow into my consoling
shroud, light folds
enfolding me: its softness
came from them.
I use it well.

SCAR

Above my left eye
        an indentation

At another new school,
a classmate threw a rock
but some angelic force
protected me:
I was not blinded.

       No memory of impact

I did not know
the stone was cast
at the same moment my mother's body
       was tossed from a bridge.
Schoolgirl hurled sharp flint into soft flesh.
Man pitched soft flesh
       onto hard rock.
       Bloodfall: stinging eye, sticky lashes,
       shock in bathroom mirror like *Carrie*.
Within the hour the girl was piggybacking me around
the playground.
       I couldn't believe my change of fortune
       so much attention (so much blood from a stone)

Did he turn away even before impact
tramping back to his car through forest full of birdsong?

Rainfall, then waterfall: rising ravine carried the body downstream.

Theory: at *his* approach, not the girl's, would my temple brand burn.
      I wait,
             standing in the stream
                    below the bridge
                          scar pulsing. I am the troll.
But he died.
In a cage.
      Protected.

LOYALTY

She has given up on spring,
the new warmth that allows us back into their realm;
believes winter is routinely unremitting
until she comes to a stop
beside the salmonberry bush, its branches
still naked, pink flowers
unfolding, fulfilling their promise,
a little ragged with rain. Soon
she is weeping copiously over them
as she does every year.

Needs the seasons
to continue their constancy
if she is to succeed in transfiguring
from keeper to beater to seeker.
With autumn's approach she sets up guard
at the goal posts of malaise, keeps
gloom at bay with constant vigilance
and repeated saves. Through winter's chilled
clutches she wraps her cloak around herself,
gets her broomstick moving, forward progression,
no pausing, and raises her bat to beat off despair.
Every hit a triumph, each year more tiring;
the rogue bludgers are burgeoning.

Then, swamp lanterns emerge from their mud
and her clouded remembrall clears: there is something
to reach for. Soon the frogs will sing,

the hummingbirds will hover and shimmer like snitches
and the wounded will dare
to sense victory again, take a chance,
stand on a speeding broom and listen
for fast wings, stretch for gold,
forgetting our scars,
having come out from behind them
a straining arm bursting with promise
like a branch, with blossoms even before leaves.
The final somersault of thanks
emerges: mouth full of spring.

CHRISTINE LOWTHER

SO WE DEAL

There are trapdoors
and then there are trapdoors;
either way, they beat detention.
Before you can even decide
whether to go through and drop down
or not, there's the three-headed dog
to deal with. And if we get past
dog and door
there's Devil's Snare
to congeal with.
But what else can you do?
Dung happens.
Earwax-flavoured beans happens.
What fate befalls
the stone maker,
rock thrower,
conscience breaker?
One wizard's weapon
is another one's balm.

AND LATER, THE HUNGRY BATS

Augusticolis again, winged
termites, herald of season's change,
summer do-se-doing with fall
around a beach bonfire.
Their first night, like someone opened the hatch
and let them all fly out at once
landing on the dogs,
riding the woodsmoke,
falling into the bag of chips,
sipping at beer cans,
balancing their burden of stiff wings
on our cheekbones.

And you see them as keys,
fluttering toward the lock on a door
you're not sure you want to open,
because it's easier to stay put,
easier
not to move on
than to reach forward
however necessarily
and touch wood.

THE STEMMER

Small hands, trembling, splayed,
life lines long, place where pen
(wand) is held callused,
ink splotches from recently
written exams,
reaching toward the ugly face of evil.
Not young against old necessarily,
but goodness reaching to stem
a flow of harm.

Yet the face comes on,
shaking hands touch malevolence
burn what has been used and wasted.
Skin dries, cracks, turns
to ash. The taste of smoke
on the tongue of the reacher,
the seeker, the stemmer.

Sounds of snarling, rasping,
undignified clinging and grasping
—a high, fast breathing
through brave sobs
crackling of flames
a hale heart beating
harder than it ever has before
and voices, finally;
a strong clear voice calling
two names with equal confidence
and determination, the voice
of help.

The stone in hand holds hidden
sorcery and philosophy;
its weight is considerable.
It has much to answer for.
Before loss of consciousness
the scent is burnt skin,
cooked fabric of a teacher's
cloak, a clearing blast of decent air
and then ... sherbet lemon.

UNSPOKEN THOUGHTS

You choose to see the best in people,
or what you'd prefer to see,
seeing is believing, believing—seeing.
How could you have been friends
with the faux flame, Flamel?
A worthy alchemist
would never have kept
that rock to himself.

II

SECRETIVE CHAMBERS: HEART AND MIND

PROOF

It's not just Malfoy, it's Crabbe and Goyle now, too
—I mean, their equivalent in my small town.
Maybe I'm just as Slytherin as they are,
did I cast the wall's warning words?
Malfoy, Mal*foy*, *malformed*,
frenemies, too weak to love
the likes of me, the seeker
of those worthy of loving,
those strong enough to love me.

Why would anyone choose evil? Power
spilling over, uncontainable
(to be contained is to be alone).
Freedom from the rules.
Forbidden fruit.
Cool clothes.
Street cred. Sexiness.
Suspicion, accusations against us:
these at least indicate notice.
But to elect hurting
people, choose killing?
I don't even like murdering slugs.
I don't even want *one* enemy.
Like Voldemort, I'm trying
to make up for being here by accident:
powerful is purposeful.
Invisible or invincible? No hesitation.
From our place of fear

we'll do anything
to make ripples,
force an impact on the lives around us,
demanding tattoos, leaving scars.
A wave of enmity is, after all,
proof.

NETWORKING

No one ever held back my mail
though I was once made to wash
purple dye out of my hair.
No bars were fitted onto my window
though I was sometimes
liberated by friends.
We imagined,
        oh, how we imagined
traveling
by green fire.

FACES

We know that look, have felt it
on our own faces, Harry's expression
as he meets the phoenix for the first time:
sweetest smile of surprised greeting,
respectful curiosity, a touch of awe,
recognition amidst his innocence,
like crossing paths in the wild
with some creature that lives there.
A new being renews innocence
in the human, any human,
even a horcrux, healing
before a single tear is shed.
The sight of us – another surprise –
sends the bird over the edge

into flame and resurrection.
Zen baby mellow in rebirth
serene in his joy
to greet again, from ashes.
What are we to make of this:
soft cinders piled
upon a fledgling's head
and under this bonnet of ruin
he lifts up a face
of easy rapture.
He's not even trying,
miraculous bird,
everything he does
is a lesson in love.

Soft chirruping sounds.

No parents: autonomous.
Effortless tranquillity,
transformative power,
deep contentment,
otherworldly beauty;
of all the attributes of Fawkes
his independence is what I most admire.
I think of that strength
and feel the features of my face
realign themselves.

SHOULDA THOUGHTA THAT

The polyjuice was such a pain,
why couldn't we have simply
crept behind someone
into the Slytherin common room
under my cloak?

FOR OUR WIDE-ARMED MOTHERS

You'll never be gone,
not as long as those who remain
are loyal to you.
What does this mean?
Not being silent,
as the cry of the phoenix attests.

The boy's mother threw her arms wide:
a blockade.
You stayed in a perilous marriage
for our sake.
Her murderer went into hiding,
yours took us away,
hid behind lies,
was caught.

The boy's friends, at least the bookish ones,
knew more about him
than he knew himself.
But who didn't?
Even the media knew more about us.
We learned from radio specials,
interviews, salvaged
tapes of past readings,
poems on paper.
He read nothing of Lily
until he held in his hands
a fragment of a letter,
sudden grief and joy *thundering*
five books later.

He was told, not soon enough,
from those outside the family
that he had his mother's eyes.
What did the rock-thrower,
my scar-maker know,
as she reached for her weapon
in the forest behind the school?
What did she believe,
what had she assumed?

> *Heard your mother's dead*
> *Heard your father killed her*
> *Why have you come to our school*
> *How come you're acting normal?*

I tried *Obliviate* on my cat;
the memory charm backfired.
I haven't a clue who I am!
but here's a promise – arms wide –
I love everybody!

The light of the body is the eye:
scar-maker, you nearly blinded me.
It's all right.
It's over.
It's just a memory.
Wasn't told until my twenties
from someone outside the family
that I had my mother's eyes.

Meanwhile the ministry

wants to log the dark forest,
Arania Exumai an unruly army
of spiders. I can't agree.
Yes, it's where the stone was thrown
but blame the forest?
I was taught well.
I will throw my arms wide:
a blockade.

DEAR DIARY

Diary, dear diary,
my confidant since I was ten,
every page as full of fully visible ink
teenaged and middle-aged angst
as I could muster without a wand:

please grant me one handful
of green powder and let me go!
You've become a chore
and there are no perks.
I have to buy or steal each new pen
without the affirming light show
that comes with a wand.
Granted, who would prefer
to repeatedly endure
Ollivander's creepy countenance?
The man is obsessed.

But diary! not so dear,
the older I get,
the longer I write,
the clearer it is:
you are no way to preserve oneself;
half a century of hiding
only to be pinned by a serpent's fang.
It's one thing to keep records,
ruminate on life's peak experiences
— another to divide the soul
into pages, flee from fortune,
believe we are above fate,
chase the immoral immortal
impossible, fraction and hate.

CHRISTINE LOWTHER

GINEVRA OF THE JOURNAL

All those long years
of slow dawning comprehension
with Mum and Dad while the others
trouped off to school,
truth was I felt like an alien.
What else is the only female
among six boys?
And some of them damn sharp-eyed.
As for Mum, God love her,
she barely let me out of her sight.
At first I went at nighttime
—took Charlie's broom,
conquered quidditch.
No underage magic was required,
a broomstick is a broomstick: magical.
But Dad found me, and we crafted
our plan to persuade Mum.
There was no need.
My mother is much more
than a mollycoddling bore.

But don't think that flying
and goal-shooting
was all I was up to.
I've been called wise beyond my years,
thought it intelligent
to use my time well
—nights in Fred and George's empty room

snooping and pondering.
It was they, the not-bookish,
who left a tome of hexes behind.
I could read, couldn't I?
Percy had taught me when I was three.

To my surprise, when my own
September the First came around
I was loathe to leave my parents.
Father had fought Lucius Malfoy:
in a *bookshop*, mind you.
I was not an innocent; I saw the journal
drop into my cauldron
with the other text and felt triumph–
Malfoy Sr. had been careless with his things
and his loss, I thought,
could only be our gain.
I loved Harry, which you know,
and looked forward to sharing
this trifling victory with him
… as soon as I found nerve enough
to open my mouth and talk to him.

Well, it was shared, all right,
but not as I had planned.
This, too, you know.
None of what occurred
was any crass attention-seeking scam;
I get enough of that
being the youngest, the only *girl*.

Being rescued by my love?
Couldn't have designed it better myself.
Except that I could. Like remembering
not to trust anything without a visible brain,
the journal, the Riddle:
yes, I blame myself.
This *girl* is no victim.
We were nearly killed,
and that gorgeous bird
had to weep onto the terrible wound.
Hell of a way to get to know someone,
too: unconscious.

Now that is all over;
it will be a while before
I can try out for the house team
so until school year ends
there is time to practise
a spell I read about in the hex text.
I'm not squeamish:
something about bat wings and bogeys.
The twisted thing is …
being possessed by that sicko
has deepened my crush to obsession.
I feel closer, now,
to the boy who lived.

WORST MEMORIES

The nine and three-quarters barrier
baulked, the anglia ran out of sap,
seven muggles saw us,
a willow whomped back.

My best friend broke his wand
and vomited slugs for hours.

An evil idiom slithered
from my own tongue.
School-wide paranoia plagued me,
pureblood mania maligned me

like that rogue ball
and the pipelining basilisk
that nearly killed me thanks to a memory
of oddment-Riddle. He enthralled Ginny.
I'd thought *I* did that.

Let's not forget whining ghosts
and deathday parties, deadly diaries,
there is more I'm forgetting;
my broken boneless arm!
Drinking essence of thug,
turning spy.

Spiders, Skelegro and serpents,
that counterfeit poser, a gilded goose
of the Locked Heart:

CHRISTINE LOWTHER

my second year
of magical instruction
sucked. Yet, I met

the mighty phoenix
who saved us.
I struck with the silver sword.

III

FREED FROM AZKABAN

CHOICE

Choose to hear the stirring music and take this ride:
aim for the sky between spire-tipped towers,
glide over water, toward the distant mountain;
all your scars blazing defiance,
blasting misery to its dungeon;
hold on and let go, the crippled and bereaved
alive and screaming with life.

> *I am hurt, but survive. Anguish, desolation, I howl*
> *with laughter at thee. Watch me,*
> *the wounded walking, the mortally injured dancing,*
> *flying in your face.*

HOME FROM HONEYDUKES

They brought back sweets but I couldn't
stomach the *fudge*,
made me think of the minister, that *scurvy cur*,
all the adults keeping me out of Hogsmeade.
My gut felt like top-floor riding on the knight bus.
At least now I know there's a place to squat
in case I ever find myself doing underage magic
again: a certain haunted Shack.
How much worse can it be than Privet Drive?
Shrieking versus Little Whinging?
I'll live as an outcast after all
safe from Ripper and Aunt Marge,
drink polyjuice and fly to London on a whim,
finally get those solid gold gobstones,
that exact model of the galaxy
serenely spinning in its sphere.

THE WRITER'S BOGGART

It might be a cliché:
a gravestone with my name on it,
weathered and wearing away, forgotten,
or my nephew, poor and diseased,
living on the street or dead;
it might appear as me, fat,
or my collected works, burning,
or worse, unadvertised,
unpromoted, unreviewed,
rotting in a landfill
unread.
Hard to know one's deepest fear:
an earthquake — the Big One
we've all been dreading;
a tsunami drowning the peninsula;
the end of oil;
a comet hurtling towards Earth.
The last rainforest cleared;
a melt-down at the nuclear power plant.

   Riddikulus!

The nuke-station is an old fashioned windmill
singing *Wheeee* gleefully as its blades turn.
The clearcut is a forest standing up from a nap;
the comet is a giant marshmallow,
a hooting snowy owl,

the ferret Draco will become;
the end of oil is the end of toil;
the tidal wave is made of chocolate;
the quake merely tickles everyone's feet.
The boggart becomes everybody
with my latest book glued open to their faces
—the one Ron said you can *never stop reading*—
promotional materials and underlined reviews
held tightly in their hands. The boggart
becomes a purple and orange
polka-dotted headstone with the words
HA! HA! HA! emblazoned permanently upon it.
The boggart becomes me, plump as Pomona,
laughing and rolling around on shrivelfigs.
The boggart becomes my nephew,
bright-eyed and rosy-cheeked,
lying in his hammock re-reading Rowling
for the hundredth time,
and, having reached manhood,
dressed in brand new authentic quidditch robes.
He's asking to be called Ludo Bagman.

THE PULSE

all it takes is one butterbeer
golden-sweet
warming as it goes down
more medicinal than Rosmerta's mead
let's drink it just to feel
the pounding of the pulse
without fear
look mortality in the face
so easy now,
so easy
to accept our ailments
the pulse is power
the pulse is fragility
there is no contradiction
softness and steel
an inside
infinitely more vast
than its shell

WHAT YOU CHOSE TO REMEMBER

You're right, I don't fancy playing quidditch
in this weather, even on a broom
with pinpoint turning;
have you ever been blown backwards
up a downslope on your bicycle?
Talk about *aresto momentum*!
But there's more to worry about than storms—
evil corporations rule the world;
good people die young.
What would winning look like?
       Reversing the impetus,
       no wand required.

Yet, you are quietly proud to realize
the knowledge exists in your mind
that a hawk with pointed wings
must be a peregrine.
Certain things you have chosen to remember,
they will all need to be released,
our own private cultures will end.
It is a hard fall to a smashed broomstick.
Be comforted: the falcon
will have entered the archway
many times before us.

CHRISTINE LOWTHER

EXPECTO PATRONUM

Sir, how am I supposed to learn this spell
when I'm not sure
I never want to hear her voice again?
I have my mother's eyes
and her voice in my skull
when evil approaches
rooting me, literally: tubers
extend underground from my feet
hooking me here,
you say an entrapment
addictive as Erised.
You've taught us about it: when wizards
become enthralled to dementors,
obsessed with our own pain,
almost unbearable, but deeply familiar to us.
Also addicting, the chocolate cure.
Muggles have twelve steps;
all we have is one: *Expecto Patronum.*
It must be very powerful. But sir
…any second now, I might hear my mother
again…shouldn't think that, or I *will*
hear her, and I don't want to,
or do I?

Listening to echoes of her won't bring her back.
We carry them around with us in our chests.
The ones who love us never really leave us.
They belong to us; we belong to them
connected eternally. Yes, that word.

SPARE BIT OF PARCHMENT

I must confess to the gambling
of your sacrifice for a bag
of magic tricks. A magic map,
to be precise.
Maybe it's the James in me,
rebel, joker,
or maybe it's that I've spent
my whole life missing out,
and now that I can,
my impulse is to *find* out,
find what, find why, find
who is roaming the halls at night
under the name of a dead man.
It was only to feel closer to you
that I went to find him.

ALL IN ONE DAY

The tear-stained parchment said
Buckbeak, Hagrid's haughty
hoofed eagle, would be executed.
When Ron offered his aid in the appeal
I fell apart, flung myself on him, blubbing.
Moments later my wand was out
—I had smacked Mal-*foul* across
his loathsome face with my bare hand. He fled.
I fell asleep from sheer exertion,
stress and grief, a taxed timetable;
slept through a lesson,
never even reached the classroom.
Next period, that flaky four-eyed *professor*
had the gall to declare
my mind *hopelessly mundane.*
I stomped out of her class, for good!
because if there is one thing I've learned
this year so far, it is
not to misuse time.

BEFORE THE DAMAGE

You could have done much more with the time-turner,
a delicate instrument more precise than any stone.
With it, you could have visited your parents
while they were still living,
killed their assassin before the damage was done,
made friends with your younger self,
gotten to know your whole family,
kept Sirius close.
How have you neither devised
nor dreamed this greatest adventure?
Take the cloak now, Chosen One,
infiltrate the ministry, it's never too late
—obviously. Find where they keep
the time-turners and seize one;
that is all we'll require.
We shall use it in turns,
be in their presence.
You may have to come back
and find me, when I will gladly
surrender its magic to you,
no longer needed;
these final instructions
I offer in case
I decide to stay.

CHRISTINE LOWTHER

IV

GOBLET OF HEALING FIRE

TRAUMA REMEDY FOR TRAVELERS

The train speeds across France to Milan,
mountains hidden in the dark,
tears evaporating on a clammy face,
sweat drying under tremoring arms.
The forgotten stone, in my pocket
all this time? Smooth stone,
jagged stone, round stone, angular:
it is just one stone. My hand suddenly
full of home, mineral flooded
with warm hard certainty;
fingers press for a portkey.
Now I know why I brought this along,
to be saved by my own forgotten precaution,
one piece of Earth preferred
over any other.
I hold it flat against my forehead,
feel its island under my feet
       steadying.

TO BE HERE

Carelessly my parents tossed in my name
: by accident, you understand me,
hurling me into the world
and now I'm not supposed to be here
unless we are all "meant" to be
…and who believes that?

I'm in a lot of trouble
with my teachers, who are everyone,
a world full of wiser-than-I,
expecting me to outwit a dragon,
come up holding the golden egg.
Do you honestly believe she'll end up free
because of me, despite my burnt hands?
The *dancing, blue-white flames*
in the goblet were called friendfyre.
Friend or fiend, I never touched them,
and still got burnt.

And I would do it again.

CHRISTINE LOWTHER

WHAT A THING TO SAY

1.
To lose one's family —
never whole again, are we?
Look, I've only just met you,
shouldn't we be chatting about the weather?
What is the appropriate response? *You are right,*
I am broken, is it that obvious?

2.
He-who-must-not-be-named
did great things – terrible, yes,
but great. Murder is great?

3.
So! No poems about you, *eh?*
Oh, *silencio*, already.
You are the only one
besides myself to notice
all her children except for me
had poems written for or about them.
I've only just met you.
How shall I reply?
Right – I guess I was her least favourite?
Or – *Yes, I was the accident,*
and so fiercely autonomous
there was no need for advice,
no need for poems.

I'm sorry I have no elucidation for you.
Not all children inspire a mother's muse.
What's YOUR excuse?

4.
Right about now I'd grab
a glob of gillyweed,
enough to spend an hour
under water, as deep as possible,
seeking solace
from the merpeople
and their spears.
Grasp of language
will not be required.

FEELING PENSIVE? a Found Poem
in J. K. Rowling's *Harry Potter and the Goblet of Fire*

Shallow stone basin
odd carvings around the edge
runes and symbols not recognized
silvery light coming from its contents
liquid or gas? Bright, whitish silver
moving ceaselessly, the surface
became ruffled like water beneath wind
or like clouds, separated and swirled smoothly;
it looked like light made liquid
or wind made solid

LARGE AS LIFE

Hagrid knows that living large
incites prejudice, persecution.
Olympe got there first;
women must aspire to being cute
and small. She would rather
deny what she is — insert "fat"
over "giant" — any excuse, preposterous
if necessary, a true falsehood,
big bones.
Ridicule, slander, even violence
will ensue; we must lie
to ourselves and the world,
bury the soul.
All that making fun of Dudders
and which Dursley transformed,
came through in the end?
Only he.

CHRISTINE LOWTHER

51

A PROMISE

Rita, I'd like a word
woman to woman,
a gossip-veiled, threatening word.
You see, I'm like Moody: wrong side
of, ahem, thirty-five
(Fred and George, where's
the *anti*-aging potion?
I'm joking, ain't no
flyer-from-death),
grumpy as get-out,
Barty Crouch got his personality right,
and Crouch Senior's too — again,
I can relate, we need control,
there are rules for this!
Did I mention that any thunder clap
will darken and swell my tattoo
until it raises from my skin in 3D?
After barking all day like the crusty
aging auror, pursing my lips
like the anal Crouch,
I might just cry like Winky,
neglect to wipe my nose,
and still watch you, Skeeter,
through the back of my head.

SOMETIMES I TALK TO MY WAND

Because life is a damn bludgering maze,
point me bloody well won't you,
pull my foot out
of the grass-covered ceiling
don't let me fall head-first
into the stars, fall away
from the world,
god, I'd rather be visiting
Snuffles and Beaky in their cave
instead of solving some smarmy
sphinx's riddle, and now worse,
Tom Riddle,
flesh, blood and bone,
my friend is dead,
the song inside me says
don't break the connection
yet that is exactly what I must do.

CHRISTINE LOWTHER

THE UNTAMED FLEEING UP TREES

Do not meet a tree
if unable to accept
leaves shaping your mind.
–Robin Skelton

...all the leaves
rushed shouting shimmering
out of my veins.
–Pat Lowther

So much pain in remembering we
were animals not human children not
girls but rabid savage *un*disciplined *over*disciplined
ungrateful corrupted spoiled manipulated
brainwashed: turned against her turned against
our own mother our own family
too much to handle monsters like him ogres
not children — beasts without hope

Until remembering my love
for animals; the adult self
always says people are animals
should be proud to call ourselves *fauna*
could aspire to certain animal-like ways of being —

We were not without humanity
too young   no skills   no other mentors
no alternative no foundation that wouldn't
cave in
　　　　somewhere deep must have been
　　　　blood of a poet

cells of a great and beautiful mind
dragging us up and out

so much distress in having to ask
was it all just flying hair and arms
teeth and tears
spankings and screams
tearing our throats?

Dogs and people sometimes catch
bears or cougars off guard
and the wild creatures
flee up trees
I was treed by neighbourhood bullies
wrote a poem about deciding to jump
bare feet on gravel
no habitat to call home

Been fighting to keep alive ever since
even when laughing at some soireé
or bush party, otherness sits on my shoulder:
the tangled hair, the mouth
always open,
corners turned down
greedy for
a dementor's kiss

I forget to go to the trees
I forget the branches
will be held down to me
that they are waiting
to fill my hands with moss

CHRISTINE LOWTHER

55

that they are waiting
to help me climb
I forget even to stand still beneath them
and pull back my sleeves,
feel my forearms filling with sap
the skin colouring emerald
    bark taking hold;
        whole body humming *fauna* into *flora*
        this time I will not jump

V

TEARS OF A PHOENIX

IN TOUCH WITH WIZARDS

They guard the wizard prison, Azkaban.
A ringing silence filled the brightly lit kitchen,
sterilized clean surfaces stinging the eyes.
An air of tense, shocking expectancy,
of things no longer lining up,
worlds merging that should be
apart, certain persons
knowing what they couldn't.

Like the time Gram looked
from me to Uncle John and said
as if looking for reassurance
and with a hint of pride,
She wants to know everything.

Like when the murder was described
on national radio just before
I had to cycle to work
through my village
where everybody
knows everybody.

LEGILIMENCY

Feeling sentimental? ... Forever whining about how
bitterly unfair your life has been? Well, it may have escaped
your notice but life isn't *fair ...* −Severus Snape

Oh Severus, skilled Occlumens,
control me, know my mind;
sever me, expertly unhinge me:
unleash my worst memories,
be severe upon me;
lash me with your desert-dry voice
scorn me
and, despite your disdain
or because of it,
restore me.

DAUGHTER

There is no poetic word for serial killer,
except perhaps *Voldemort*.
Another nightmare woke me, seeping sweat,
the lunging, biting snake was me,
reptilian skin clammy, soul bloodless, throat heaving—
how could I ever, in good conscience,
attack a redhead? —
I was rushed to the principal's office.
Assigned a counsellor.
But I'm an innocent, I protested,
born to someone I'd never choose.
Waited for succor, reassurance…
instead she pulled me down the cold
stone spiral staircase that wound serpentine
like circling a drain,
locked me in a stuffy doily-festooned dungeon
to be Veritaserum'd with sneakoscopes,
make sure I wasn't weakening:
        wasn't becoming my father's daughter
        that the horcrux wasn't directing my mind—
You're wasting time trying to find a nonexistent weapon
I've got more important things to do
the death eaters are still logging thousand-year-old trees
in a bereft muggle world, we need a powerful shield charm!
This counsellor/henchman, it turns out, was a spy
sending copies of my best schoolwork
to my father in prison
(where there were no dementors and he thrived
on the close attention offered in maximum security)

What graver betrayal from a highschool shrink?
I came to you for guidance
you took my hand in your fist
and led me down, down the cold
hard dizzying *confunding* staircase
at your mercy

What you didn't count on was the secret practice
in my Room of Requirement, learning
how to kill red tape:
       Make it a powerful memory,
       the happiest you can remember.
       Allow it to fill you up.
       Stay focussed.
or that I'd grow up and seek justice,
send an owl or two to your current employer,
headmaster at another school
full of trusting kids.

CHRISTINE LOWTHER

BAD GIRLS BOND

Our clans were challenged as hell,
sure, but they never hung
family-tree tapestries, scorched
off faces of the disowned.

Served a grade 12 suspension
in the library with no Restricted section,
would have appreciated an advance
guard. Pally principal agreed
to put me there with her, the other
similarly troubled youth,
our families none the wiser.
No skiving snackboxes in our time;
April and I had been seen riding
the edge of the school roof.
We served our sentences giggling.

REAL, HONORABLE LIFE

It's one thing to be emotionally moved
by a rag-tag army of youth
daring, in secret, to defend themselves
against evil
—and that's just it, there has to be
a menacing enemy;
this works on screens and in books
but in life the foe is mediocrity,
smallmindedness,
discourteous treatment,
disappointing behaviour
usually coming from the self,
the struggle to make ends meet,
working in a hated job,
years of stress turning us grey.
These enemies are not movingly fought,
such rebelliousness not admired but discouraged,
or merely blinked at like a crow
with a piece of our toast in its bill.
Once Voldemort is dead and gone,
even if he was your father,
you are no longer the chosen one,
you are a dark wizard-catcher
like everyone else.

MELLIFERA

My patronus used to be a red fox;
for those years I could speak Vulpetongue.
When it changed to a harbour seal
I found myself speaking Vitulina.
The North American name for patronus
might be *totem animal*. There is nothing wrong,
I meant to say, with snakes; remember our friend
behind the glass at London Zoo.
Any Parseltongue, too, could converse
with all three heads of a Runespoor,
or expend an Ashwinder's life in one hour.
Salamanders are just as mysterious,
feeding on flame. I knew
an Aniedemouth; he spoke only
to the wandering salamander,
but what they talked of, I know not.
I saw the creatures' feet;
they looked like tiny hands.
I knew a graceful girl who spoke Cygnini;
her patronus was a swan
whose wings whistled when it flew.
Then there was the goth
who knew ravens and spoke Corvustongue.
I beg my next patronus will allow me
to speak Mellifera; I will respectfully
and in awe address the native bee,
thanking it for honeying me against bitterness,
for stinging the nose of depression.

How can I speak a different language without knowing it?
The same way we all harbour and change patronuses
without knowing them, until we learn
the spell: it is simple magic, full of wonder.

Harry – Stag – Cervumouth
Hermione – European river otter – Lutramouth
(North American river otter: Lontramouth)
Ron – Jack Russell Terrier – Echandomouth
Neville – uncertain, possibly European badger –
Melemouth
Ginny – horse – Equumouth. Ginny is blessed, for she
can also communicate with thestrals, other winged
horses, hippogriffs, porlocks and even unicorns. She can
also converse with centaurs of any nationality.
Luna – hare - Lepumouth

NEVILLE, UNLIKELY REBEL

The rain slides down a window
like the tears from Neville's eyes
when he's alone, thinking of his parents.
From his first time on a broom, disastrous,
and his ride with cornish pixies (freshly caught)
they knew he was sensitive, a little low
on self-esteem. The one time they saw
Neville nettled
they body-bound him for his bravery.
He won them the house cup.
May all the Nevilles of the world,
wizard and muggle,
be proud.
          Longbottom,
    broomsticks are for jocks.
    You look a little like my nephew.
    You conquered that boggart, dear,
    put Snape in Gran's clothing,
    you *exploded* him, Neville!
They figured later, by the way,
the more of the old fraud's teacups
he broke, the better.
Who had the best time at the Yule Ball?
    Put on your dancing shoes again, Neville,
    it was good to see you like that.
    How were you to know a plant
    would squirt so much stinksap?
    Did that stop you loving herbology?
No. Steadfast 'til the end, that's him,
stubbornly insisting he help.

Still spends every Christmas
on the closed ward at St Mungo's.
This unobvious hero coped with Snape,
leg-locker, *tarantallegra*, broken nose,
even cruciatus from that hell-witch.
Nev will help lead the re-formed
Dumbledore's Army (still recruiting).
He'll rise from his seat on the train
and address death eaters: *Hey losers!*
He'll make a home for rebels
in the Room of Requirement,
a place to hide in an unfriendly
Hogwarts, a headquarters
from which to rally and fight.

CHRISTINE LOWTHER

STEPPING OUT

A small regiment from Dumbledore's Army
travels by thestral and arrives at the ministry.
The elevator doors slide open;
the cool, bureaucratic, supremely polite voice,
a precise opposite to the situation,
calmly and neutrally announces
     Department of Mysteries.
There was a tiny pause after "department";
perhaps she's not so neutral after all,
maybe there's a bit of sarcasm there,
or a bit of "You have no idea what you're getting into.
Good luck. Ha, ha, ha."
Ginny, Neville, Luna, Harry, Ron, Hermione:
what a scraggle of misfits (well, Ginny's quite popular).
Yet all brave enough to face possible death,
the ultimate mystery.
At the department of fear, uncertainty and danger
(you can bet Mrs. Weasley's clock at home
has Ron's hand pointing to Mortal Peril now)
the voice of the ministry is efficient and bland;
the young people, wands at the ready,
     step out of the lift.

VI

HALF-BLOOD, MUDBLOOD

REPORT CARD –
ORDINARY WIZARDING LEVEL (O.W.L.)

Astronomy
Mars is bright tonight.

Care of Magical Creatures
We're condoning house-elves as unpaid servants.
It must be pointed out
that the tri-wizard tournament
promoted terrorism
against mother-dragons,
traumatizing them as they fought
to protect their eggs.
All school meals continue to favour the carnivore.
(The good marks came when I convinced
the Whomping Willow to stop squashing birds.)

Charms
Like Harry, dunno whether I want to be
with people or not;
whenever there's company I want to get away,
whenever I'm alone, I want company.
Apart from casting a patronus (see below)
cheering charms have proven most useful.
No chocolate or alcohol required!

Defence Against the Dark Arts
I don't go looking for trouble; it finds me.
On the news a five-year-old watched his father
murder and bury his mother;
guess who's doubled over suddenly
crying so hard I'm gagging?

EXPECTO PATRONUM.
My skin wants to turn inside-out,
the inside always being
greater than the outside.
There can be no art to murder,
just a darkness that spreads poison
with few antidotes; the world cup
and a roomy tent with the Weasleys works.
We need defences against negativity above all,
the patronus is a kind of positive force:
select your happy memory
(Draco as Ferret), send resentment
and horror packing.
Utilize tears, and concentrate.
Defend against silencing,
denial, oppression, despair.
What is grief, but love?
What is guilt, but love?
What is courage, but love?
What is conscience, but love?

Divination
Mars is bright tonight.

Herbology
What can I tell you? Venomous Tentacula
leaves can fetch ten galleons to the right buyer.
Some misguided wizard is breeding
gravity-resistant trees;
if he were to mate them
with flesh-eating ones ...

CHRISTINE LOWTHER

71

I take a small dose of hellebore weekly
to encourage sanity.
Have you noticed that mandrake,
though its roots are a handful,
has lovely flowers?
All right, this is not my best subject,
and there was that time I stole
the fanged geranium.

History of Magic
I always went to Florean Fortescue for help
—meaning sundaes, which had enough sugar
and caffeine to carry me through the dullest
essay. Mr. Fortescue had no equal
in Diagon, Knockturn Alley or Hogsmeade.
He made my sundaes with almond milk.
He recommended *The Mists of Avalon*.

Potions
Again with the vegetarian-challenged.
We won't use eye of human
so why eye of newt?
It's like dissection in muggle science class:
splayed frog, pig embryo.
Conscientious objector flunks.

Transfiguration
Girl to woman in seconds flat: most impressive.
Full marks.
Age thirteen. Wasn't imagining after all

the posters of a newly-deceased John Lennon
moving and talking to me.
Young woman to "mature" woman:
stout as Sprout —
holy slughorn, where's the potion for this?
Reducio! ... didn't work.
Every waistcoat button about to burst.
Nervy, but no Minerva,
and no Veela neither.

ALL THE JINXED DEFENSE TEACHERS

Quirrell gave stammerers a bad name
and turbans (forgive me) a bad rap.
He was so mean he made a troll
an innocent pawn.

Someone should have told Mr. Me
what's gilded isn't gold,
should have asked him
to unlock his heart.
Someone probably did,
probably several someones,
and then they forgot.

Loony loopy Lupin
shoved *Waddiwasi* up Peeves'
nose: thus his esteem rose,
despite his ragged clothes.
He knew about dementors,
chocolate, boggarts,
the terror of a full moon;
neglected the textbook chapter
on werewolves.
Knew about wanting to save
his family from himself.

Polyjuiced Mad-Eye Crouch?
The least said the better.
Foul servant with enough power

to fool the flaming goblet
and Dumbledore himself.
Pucker up, fiend!

The Toad came from a workplace
where staff, instead of punching the clock,
flushed themselves down a toilet.
Just two more words:
fascist bureaucrat.

But now this: Snape.
Listen to him: *The Dark Arts
are many, varied, ever-changing
and eternal. ...
You are fighting that which is unfixed,
mutating, indestructible.*
Merlin's pants!
His voice caresses what's wicked.
Snivellus was a peril in Potions
—he'll be a death eater in Defense.
We're doomed.

LIGHT AND DARK

The world isn't split into good people and death eaters; we've all got both light and dark inside of us. —Sirius Black

Some days we feel like Snape, like
not washing our hair, like leaving it
unclean for a week. Like donning
our sinister, swirling black robes
and approaching our enemies with twitching fingers,
both hands clawed and restless to close around a throat
or raise a wand and strike.
        Maybe it's just me, but some days
        I would open my mouth, utter *Sectumsempra*
        and be done with it.
        Sometimes there is honour in revenge.
        Clutching my cloak around me,
        drawing it to my breast
        with sneering self-assurance,
        leaving my enemy in the requisite pool of blood.
        Neville's worth twelve of him!
        Eat death, Malfoy!

Other days we might as well be called Luna Lovegood,
we're all about cleaning the nargles
out of everyone's ears if they'll let us.
We'll walk barefoot through fallen leaves
to visit some neglected creature.
The rain dripping from salal leaves
brings nature-lovin' tears to our eyes,

and when we touch a leaf, feel
its smooth, cold, wet greenness
we feel like Harry did when his wand chose him,
when his wand *found* him; we've been
found by the leaf, selected, singled out,
a light glows around the leaf, its branch,
and us: hair lifts from scalp.
Broadleafed moonlight blazes.
We've been discovered by salal.

So where will we choose to spend our time,
Diagon Alley or Knockturn Alley?
Oh, to live without straight lines
nocturnally, like predators,
for the dark and the stars,
all lines blurred or obliterated,
no more colours, just moods,
inclination and choice.
            To be finally caught and tamed
            by the handsome Auror.

UN-HIDE   An unashamed rant

If I can't dance, I don't want to be part of your revolution.
– Emma Goldman

It is every body's birthright: to move,
express music's ecstatic knowing.

The likes of Riddle'll kill us if we don't cry Riddikulus.

That clepto will claim us if we self-sabotage
our apprenticeship to the absurd.

If we care too much about Cool or Hot
he'll squash us. If we don't laugh as hard and as often
as we dare at fear. Fear of loving, aging,
losing our charms,

fear of going dancing after forty,
fear of going dancing alone,
fear of ageism, fear of older people,
fear of younger people, fear of prettier people,
fear of uglier people, fear of fatter people,
fear of thinner people, fear of differently
coloured/ sexed/ abled/ educated/
waged/ housed/ languaged/ aged people.

If we are embarrassing our teenaged children
we're on the right track.
They are just waking up to our seasoned world;
we've seen so much, and know how much there is
yet to see, and know we can never

possibly see or know it all.
See? We *do* know stuff.

When the dominating current shushes us,
tries to throw its invisibility cloak over us,
swim upstream: bright, eye-catching.
It's what we've been doing.
It's why we're so fit.

All of those disapproving looks directed at us
are a reminder that we must
be doing something right.

Rowling's treatise on tolerance: does it include age?

The older we *grow*, the more our souls hum,
a frenzied hidden aliveness.

ECO-WIZARDRY

Those muggles with their technology
electro magnetic emission from cell phones
wireless internet disturbing bees
and harming trees; they can make a rocket
and a jet plane. Broom, disapparition,
hippogriff or thestral, we're carbon-free.

BRIEF CORRESPONDENCES

1.
I'd like to know more about my mother.
What was she like, as
a person,
a woman,
a friend?

No, I will not share my recollections or anecdotes.
Your asking throws a dungbomb amongst them.
My memory must not be tampered with.
You want it neat: silvery threads drawn out
by wand, stored in a flask, corked,
handed over to someone I've never met,
daughter or not. Indeed, you would have me
put a stopper in death. I hope you
find the help you obviously need
and get over it.

Get over what?

She gave me her life,
but you won't give me a memory.

2.
Yes. Oh, yes. I knew her.
Your mother was there for me
at a time when no one else was.
Not only was she a singularly gifted poet,
she was also an uncommonly kind woman.
She had a way of seeing the beauty in others

even, and perhaps most especially,
when that person could not see it in himself.

3.
We have a right to our mothers,
to claim and reclaim them,
to listen for their echoes,
to articulate our grief;
we do not escape our beginning;
if our pain brings up the pain of others
we may be blamed, named.
Silence, covering up, shooing away—
these disregard the memory
of she who once lived.
The censoring voices
inside and out
are our death eaters.

4.
It was you, *unfailingly kind.*
You were the true scar-maker.
Your loving sacrifice caught the rock
hurriedly *confunded* it to veer slightly,
enough to miss the eye
and ding the temple instead,
teach me to look out,
wake up,
be the consummate survivor.

CHRISTINE LOWTHER

81

THE CAVE

Hugged by stone closing in closing out
the boisterous waves behind
there is a seaweed that stains red
the rock's every crevice
so that the tide-worn outcrop looks
like it's starting to bleed *so crude*
always about blood
that fast trickle
into sand.

Yes, this is the place;
it has known magic.

The half-blood can sense it
but is unable to visualize,
wishing for a shard of mirror
that divine glass.

Follows her own footsteps
to the smorgasbord of cuorduroy-
shelled mussels, their palaces
of blind barnacles.

So many sharp edges; as long
as aftershocks threaten
to engorge the tide
it is a risk coming
but she could never give up
this place, even temporarily.

Barnacles spread out along the rockface
like honeycombs;
hail splinters the sunshine:
sparks from a wand.

Only when she walks beside stone
can she hear the tread of her own
footsteps; otherwise, the sand or sea
swallows the sound of her.

All the locales we're not supposed to go
the Hardknock Alleys of every city
the dark forests
locked chambers, secret passageways
the maze where the open field used to be
Come-and-Go rooms
ocean caves
wherever the magic is unbridled
she would go there first.

CHRISTINE LOWTHER

THE SPLINCHED STAY

every memorial feels like the heart
engulfing the rest of the body,
this freckled four-limbed automaton
taking its place in a hard chair
lost in rows of grief, hard
as rock pounded by ocean,
the heart overwhelming,
the body sinking and drowning

through the roar the ears pick up
Who would like to share a funny memory?

      nobility of spirit
          nitwit
      intellectual contribution
          oddment
      greatness of heart
          blubber
              tweak
      something in Mermish
      a sentence in centaurian
      tribute arrows loosed

but what can be said,
where are the words of comfort
to those left behind, splinched
from the beloved's side...
great gulping gurdyroots, can't articulate—
gotta say something, no one else is rising—
the boy with long-lashed, almond eyes
loved catching frogs

the man with the dazzling smile
was a deft hand at small plane engines
silence

      She was once so distracted
      as to ladle soup onto a platter
      instead of a bowl
      and upon realizing her mistake
      carried that precarious plate
      around laughing, had to
      show everybody

      He was rare in his generation,
      a kind, handsome pilot
      I barely knew who heard
      my age and remarked sincerely,
      Girl! you are lookin' good!

      She loved Winnie the Pooh
      and thought to ask, at eight years old,
      Dad, are you a sedentary man?

laughing through tears
crying from a smile
there is more
there had to be more
but I couldn't remember
watching helplessly
as the paintings are taken down
to be put, closed, covered,
in that terrible place,
Away

VULNERA SANENTUR

What makes a bully who has taken over
where his nefarious father left off
hold a tiny white feather
up to the light and gaze upon it
rather than simply brush it from his robes?
The silken soft sorrow of the white bird
almost more beautiful in death than in life,
as if painted, lovingly,
on the wood of the cabinet
the very shadows of its feathers as sad as beauty,
as beautiful as sadness,
bewildering as a thug weeping
when he finds grief inside himself,
soft and vulnerable as the bird.
Having made all the wrong choices,
boy became bully. But this time,
no decision,
surprised by beautiful tears.

VII

EMBRACING THE HALLOWS OF DEATH

COMPARISON

The dark lord's father disowned him
My father's father beat him

Their views were extreme,
my father landing in prison
for radical leftism in the McCarthy era
the dark lord his political opposite,
cut away the canker that infects us
until only those of true blood remain

They desecrated beautiful wild places

Declared no remorse

Distorted truth,
excelled in denial

Worked alone — killed alone,
yet thrived on attention
insisted on leading others
into darkness, corrupted innocence
annihilated goodness
and also failed to bring down
the strong and virtuous

They were unusually intelligent

Death relieved us when he took them
for his own, what else could we do
but celebrate, let loose

to the point of carelessness
transfigure bitter ruination
to a downpour of shooting stars
a squall of unhidden owls in daytime

Now we want to forget them
but need to understand
maintain, in honour of their victims,
constant vigilance

OLIVE BRANCH

How many times have I read it,
the chapter that rids us of the Dursleys
once and for all? But this time
Dudley's olive branch made me
throw down the book,
slide unease along the shelf,
head for the telephone
determined to know
once and for all
if my aunt wasn't speaking to me
or what — my cousin
not answering emails —
it's the writer's risk,
publish what's true, not pretty
and make people you care about
mad. My phone card had expired.

CHRISTINE LOWTHER

HELL OF AN ALL-NIGHT CAFÉ

I was dreaming of feeding toast
to a talking head in the café's fireplace
only it was a woodstove
with its door open
(we don't have fireplaces
on the west coast)

it stopped chewing at the sight
of something past me
out the window:
a dark mark in the sky!
only it was the head
of a pink kitten
in a frilly pink collar
the gum-chewing waitress
must have been caught dodging red tape
by Delores (to cast the mark,
the incantation, neither shouted
nor whispered, never silent,
is simpered: *Prim-and-Proper!*)

I had thought the waitress was a muggle
why would a witch take orders
on the night shift
serving burly workmen
whose wands dropped sharply
from up their sleeves

or was that another dream
I meet her more often, you see,
in my sleep than daily life

always admired her stylish outfits
now guessing they've been
dress robes all along
(and not all *long*, some are
scandalously short, yet chic)

hopefully she'll be let off with a warning
the Um-bitch will believe
my waitress, who is in truth
the café owner, was imperiused
perhaps by the toast eater,
protego at the ready
in case he tries it on me
instructions: *infiltrate the ministry*
rob Gringotts
hypnotize Bogrod
set free and ride a blind dragon

such loony, loopy dreams
treasure that replicates but also burns
at the touch
a skrewt would be kinder to face
than one's own or others'
brains and their tentacles of thought
I feel like
the ghoul in pyjamas
whose howling would fit in well
on the west coast

easier to swallow soggy toast
another greyish cappuccino
than sleep

CHRISTINE LOWTHER

91

THE LIMESTONE PLAIN

The skylark sings high above Hermione
seated upon her peaceful plain of stone
sings high though a girl's heart below is low
with the weight of her parents' memories
and the absence of her angry love.
On Malham Cove limestone she studies the signs,
carries out what she always does: her duty,
hoping to do some good in the world,
whatever is true and within her power.
She means to find meaning
in a children's fable,
make the signs plain.
And the lark sings high above Hermione
seated on her peaceful plain of stone.

THE PUT-OUTER

Ever been told to lighten up?
Well, hear this:
                    Darken down.
Quit giving the darkness a bad rap.
Dumbledore himself
created the delicious deluminator.
No mistake
that collecting light
to create darkness
was merely its day-job.

Note that the listening-in light
was not dazzling and white, but
a ball of light, kind of pulsing, and bluish
like a Portkey's.
Love whispers our name in the dark;
we know to follow then.

When leaves fall to cover the ground
parts of the world become hidden,
the glare is softened,
quiet descends.
Life is made in the dark;
let *lumos* lie sleeping.
We are productive, undistracted
out of the sun. The mind grows
fertile, ideas take shape, wisdom looms.
In the darkness of digging a friend's grave
is the agony where lucidity blooms.

Try crawling under a boulder;
there may be other fascinating life forms
waiting there. Our senses other than sight
will intensify, clarify. It may be safe
to hide here for a while, until
we allow the self to hear love
whispering our name.
Then there will be strength enough
to emerge, stand in the light,
know the next step.
We will have made our best choice
in the dark.

CHRISTINE LOWTHER

THE DOE a Found Poem
by JK Rowling in *Harry Potter and the Deathly Hallows*

silver-white doe
moon-bright and dazzling
picking her way over the ground
still silent
leaving no hoof prints
in the fine powdering of snow

she stepped towards him
her beautiful head
with its wide, long-lashed eyes
held high

inexplicable familiarity
he had been waiting for her
they had arranged to meet
she had come for him
and him alone

deeper into the forest
she led him

LONG GAME ENDED, TIME TO LEAVE THE AIR

*And what is to cease breathing, but to free the breath from
its restless tides, that it may rise and expand and seek God
unencumbered?* –Kahlil Gibran

1.
Ain't wearing no horcrux accessory
to blame the melancholic mood on.
Why does death feel like a betrayal
after we've been aware of its lifelong
companionship since we first
discovered it or were told?
–Where's your dad, Mummy?
–He's dead, son.
–Like a bug?
Yes, like an insect,
tumbled away like miniscule flotsam
irretrievable, either by priori incantatum
or resurrection stone.
Without faith, is there only
–Son, one day you will be erased?
Photographs of the diseased bring only
stabs of pain, a sinking nausea,
did they cut off all her long hair
before cremation or did that burn too?
Does her lover keep some in a locket
around his neck or safe in a chest,
or is this now considered
morbid? Still alive in pictures,
robust with health, round and rosy;
imagine now

CHRISTINE LOWTHER

a profound stillness,
the pale eyes closed,
the sealed mouth indifferent,
the bones crumbled by cancer,
    Episkey!
cannot mend, cannot reform
nor hold together, hold to us.
Some kind of unforgivable theft is here,
to take her from the world and the world
from her, pictures and ashes the only evidence.
Pictures that do not move
because death won't budge.

2.
Tempests rear up and howl
when spring encroaches onto winter's
territory; it doesn't want to die either.
The ferns, huckleberry bushes and salal
seem to crowd in close
whenever I'm preoccupied with death.
        We are at the mercy of plants.
Everyone I've loved who has died
appears in my dreaming as Petrified,
in need only of a little mandrake potion.
Mandragora, that there had been time
to caress my beloveds' faces
with your white-green flowers,
peduncles nodding life into stone,
life into death, renewal into bone.
Instead, their faces are consumed
by the storm, made still
like the dead of winter,
bloom or fade, they won't look.

And where does the phoenix go,
singing its *stricken lament of terrible beauty*,
its music coming from inside us,
our grief *turned magically to song*
soaring away on flame-bright wings?

3.
... somebody somewhere is tryin' to breathe ... –Tears for Fears

After the memorial I researched
famous poems about Death, considered
that everything is the way it is
because of him.
This seeker would covet the snitch
for its resurrection stone, more than
the bereaved stretch for reconciliation,
dream of reunion, *Let them swim*
in the deepest ocean
or glide over the highest cloud
: I would turn away from dreams,
deny closure, strive for an opening
at the close. *Am I meant to know,*
but not to seek?

Friends, siblings, teachers die,
teens commit suicide, elders wither,
cancer claims all ages, offering us
to Death in his invisibility cloak,
the one and only, named also Dread,
maimer, healer. To be sure,
we'll cast off the cloak
(borrowed or inherited),
and greet Death like an old friend.

CHRISTINE LOWTHER

97

But will we go with him gladly,
walk calmly into Death's arms
departing this life as equals,
let him grasp us about the waist
and take flight on those
great, black wings?
What happened to *the last enemy*
that shall be destroyed?

The stories strike harder and harder
as the universe calculates our growing
capacity to meet anguish with joy,
to master not death but pain,
dance despite our scars' burning.
Surrounded, yet unwilling to look:
no wonder thestrals have not materialized.
One by one our guardians stand to protect us
only to fall; not even the shelter
of a parent's arms can save us.
You strengthen and weaken us
with repeated blows, Death.

Can we hear them,
just behind the veil?

Death of parents defines whole lives.
Death of the godfather triggered resentment.
Death of the mentor added a clean hopelessness.
Death of the familiar snapped a last link.
Death of the warrior brought shock and reminder.
Death of the elf keened a clear, wrenching sorrow.
Death of the brother wrung bitter refusal.
Death of the child repeated rejection.

Death of the wolf, of the metamorphmagus,
a declared blindness, a rewriting of the story.

4.
Love is stronger than darkness
Love is stronger than death
   −Bruce Cockburn

The writer, and this is just an opinion,
was at all times reaching out to Death.
         The books are what they are because she died
         —because I loved her and she died.
She sought an understanding
even a friendship
with that lifelong companion.
To succeed, to arrive at such a juncture—
feel her hand closing over the mere possibility—
she had to release hope again and again,
aim it at all of us,
throw it as high as she could, because sure
we're all in this doxy-swarm together,
we all get bludgered despite dodging,
and when we swerve and fall, see stars,
she probably wondered if she'd ever rise
and mount her broom again.
The hands led her; they
kept on, always in motion.

5.
A boulder's quartz arteries
like lightning rods
threads of time
half sunk in wet sand
veins on a penis
crackling of a spell
from a wand
There are valleys in between
the wider threads, I can't help it
I want the rock to crack asunder
and tell me there's life ongoing
that they knew they were leaving
that there was the deepest,
most firmly declared knowing.
There is all the difference in the world
between being dragged into that arena
and walking in, if I could, with head held high.
When my own time comes I want to know,
damn it, you make sure
I'll know.

NEW WORLD WANDS
(Wandlore, Part 2)

Who is surprised now, Ollivander?
Student has become teacher
and those seldom-blinking eyes of yours
show clear astonishment.

Tell us you haven't yet retired.
There are exciting new materials
for wands in the new world,
just ask the Salem witches.
Turtle Island, North America,
Canada: the wizards here
are staggeringly powerful,
harness the muscle of aurora borealis
with wands of ancient wood,
and no trees die for them.
Thousand-year-old cedar, spruce and fir wands
encase Marbled Murrelet feather cores,
the plumes collected from rainforest floors
far beneath this endangered sea bird's nest.
Salmonberry and salal wood wands
hide black bear fur cores.
Hemlock and sequoia swish and flick
with centres of sasquatch hair.
You must come. Be prepared to work.
Build up your strength first;
even you-know-who
would have been out of his element here.

CHRISTINE LOWTHER

THE MOLLY

Jury's still out on whether your triumph over Bellatrix
makes up for your gender-traditional role.
Yet you are the Molly we love,
the mother we love,
motherly love.

Substitute, stand-in mum, adopted mother,
mine's name was Hilary, had six of her own
already, zero hesitation in taking me
under her wing, fluffing her feathers
to make sure I was comfortable there. Like Molly

she loaded up my plate with good food.
"Nothing shocks me," she said, and heard
my story. Her home was unusual:
everyone there seemed to like me.
She was the Molly we love, the mother we love,
motherly love.

Your heart is honey, your backbone steel.
You took us in when your house
was already full, fed us what we needed.
Don't let those boggarts get the better of you.
The best: the Molly we love, mother we love,
motherly love.

THE WEREWOLF

Remus, the name a poem
Lupin, the name a flower
protecting us from the archway
your dearest friend fell through:
every word you uttered
caused you physical pain

In the yard, your face
was set and white
behind its scratches and scars
you seemed unable to speak
that muscle jumping
in your jaw

Remus, tender and sensitive
wise teacher, brooding friend
ecstatic father
your youth cut short
your life hard-won
kept learning, continued loving
to the bitter end

We howl for you

CHRISTINE LOWTHER

KENDRA'S THANKS

Ariana of the air
she was fair, she was faerie, toes
never touched the ground.
Aberforth her anchor,
our goated, earth element.
Albus was ambitious.

Now the anchor alone survives,
steel, but a little rusty,
stubborn in the face
of imminent war.
You heard him: anger
and grief came at you
from straight off his chest.
And by hearing, freed him,
threw your faith
against that chain,
dislodged him,
it was as if he'd heard
a direct call:
        Aberforth, come forth!

LORD THINGY
or What Ron Sang to his Children at Bedtime

Unworthy of the dark,
wilfully ignorant,
stubborn and grim,
let's call him Dim.
The Dim Lord!
Stupid to ignore
and underestimate love,
let's call him Daft.
The Daft Lord!
What a fiend,
meanest bully in the schoolyard,
absolute prick,
let's call him Shaft.
The Shaft Lord!
Puffed-up popinjay
such self-import,
the mystique of being *bad*,
let's call him Sad.
The Sad, Sad Lord!

CHRISTINE LOWTHER

LONGBOTTOM LEAF

He likes to tell his students,
"There is no *hideous* in *Orchideous*."
They laugh and conjure bouquets,
ask about the old days,
beg to see his D.A. coins.
He doesn't like to talk about
what it felt like under the burning hat,
how he sliced off the snake's head
with Gryffindor's sudden sword,
how heavy were the bodies he carried,
how many of his friends died.
When they ask him
what kind of scholar he was,
he assures them: "The worst.
I was forgetful, a klutz,
slow and untalented
besotted by plants."
They want to know, naturally,
how such a student became a teacher.
The other professors say
he reached a certain point
and visibly hardened,
birthed an unequalled determination,
that a strange light glowed in his eyes,
that these changes made
for a beautiful thing to behold,
that Neville, a most unremarkable child,
in his striving revealed his nobility.

The professor himself has quietly offered
that it was revenge at first,
stubborn, sweaty, hard work,
relentless repetition slow to reward;
that his passion and practice
were in tribute to his parents.
With a mass escape from Azkaban
this work became preparation. As a bonus,
it got the grandmother off his case.

He does not speak of bringing Greyback down.
His daily reward lies in watching
pupils' hard work pay off.
Professor Longbottom is too modest to say it:
this plain boy became a great wizard,
one who killed anger,
guided love to father his every action.

A BOY'S HANDS

It was with those hands that he stroked Hedwig,
sometimes absent-mindedly,
having swiped frantically
at a fountain of airborne letters,
clutched a train ticket to a new life
his holly and phoenix feather wand
never far from those fingers.
And those hands hung
from a shaking, bewitched broomstick
only to proudly hold up his first snitch
to a riotously cheering crowd.

He laid those hands flat
against a magic mirror
hoping to fall through the glass
and reach his family, hands
that pulled a blood-red stone from his pocket,
pressed a painful forehead scar.

Even his young hands were those
that burned Quirrell,
vanquished Voldemort.

The caring hands
that protected Dobby from himself
opened and thumbed through an empty diary
before making their own ink offering.

And those the brave hands
that killed a monster with the sword of Gryffindor
took up the basilisk fang
to spear the horcrux pages.

Those neglected, vigorous hands
clutched a Hogsmeade permission form,
held a grim teacup,
let go of a flying hippogriff's neck.

How many times did his hands
open and close the Marauder's Map?
Write to Padfoot?
Raise his wand to cast his father's patronus?

Amazing to think of such hands, teenaged,
gripping the perilous connecting
thread between two wands
refusing to let go of Cedric
and, a quieter time, humbly stroking Fawkes
or tenderly replacing the fallen
framed picture of his parents.

Remember in your mind the hands
bleeding with Umbridge's torture,
gripping Neville's arm in congratulations
for his first, hard-won stunning spell,
being pulled roughly down a spiral staircase,
holding high a glass prophesy,
carrying low a worn potions textbook.

The hands that found and administered the bezoar
to save a friend's life
also cast the slicing spell
that bled an enemy classmate,

but would later pull that enemy
out of fire, save him from death.
One hand steadied Slughorn's
as the professor, shaking,
transferred his memory into a tiny flask;
the other's light touch caused Morvolo's horcrux-ring
to spin wildly on Dumbledore's desk.

These hands were put upon.
Forced to tip potion into a beloved
headmaster's tortured mouth.
Hexed to be still while this mentor
fell under attack.

But they felt the smooth, soft salve
of the invisibility cloak
sliding through their fingers
the cloth supple as water, light as air.
They never sought or clung to power,
but buried Moody's eye.

Even these hands, that wrested
three wands from the hands of Draco
and thereby cast a triple spell,
even these that craved the Elder Wand
buried their saviour *properly: without magic.*
These hands dug *with a kind of fury,*
relishing the non-magic of it,
every blister Harry's offering to the elf.
These very hands turned over the stone
three times, and brought back the dead.
Then let the stone go.

These hands, legendary, persevered
with the unerring skill of the seeker
stopped the last killing curse
and caught the Elder Wand, but chose
to mend the holly wand

and let the Deathstick go.

GINNY

Still the only other to have been possessed,
who got left behind, nevertheless,
and made to attend a school
with death-eater professors?
He tried to keep me from fighting,
he takes it for granted that I'll wait,
be here to talk to for years;
he leaves me with my head
on my mother's shoulder
and seeks his servant,
a sandwich,
and sleep.
You might say, *fair enough!*
and frankly, I agree.
It suits me, in truth:
this heart is fully occupied
with grief for my brother Fred,
ah, my beloved brothers,
alas, poor George,
my poor parents,
our poor Percy. Merlin save us
from such pain, such wrong,
how will we ever laugh again.
My heroes this year
have been Tonks, rest in peace,
and Luna – I love her –
but Molly, my mother,

I will not leave her now,
my blessed, brave,
devastated,
devastating
breathtaking
mother.

STARTING NOW

An engaging equivalent to the Vulcan katra,
an individual's preserved essence:
moving, talking portraits of the deceased.
Alas for the poor muggles, no paintings,
no ghosts; all they have learned dies with them,
all they have become, their very evolution
they must let go. Even as they sense
Death approaching, unanticipated
power swells to their pores,
this division the most natural milestone
in life: body and self must disengage
their embrace. The grandmother
with house full of clocks is relieved
of them by a burglar. He leaves
untouched her dozens of mirrors.
Goodbye and farewell
are the only words left.
There is just one choice:
to listen deeply to each other.

CHRISTINE LOWTHER

ACKNOWLEDGMENTS

My thanks,

To the living:

Joanne Rowling
Robert Trexler
Warner Brothers
Travis Prinzi and the contributors to:
    Hog's Head Conversations: Essays on Harry Potter
John Granger
Hilary McKernan
Vera and Tim Webb
Ursula Vaira
Beth Wilks, Rowan & Chris Jang
Jeanette Embury
Katie-Jo and Deb Crocker
Adrienne Mason, Patrice & Ava Hansen
Warren Rudd
Corinne Murray
Keith Harrison
Kathleen Shaw
Anita Sinner
Rafe Mair
Sherry Blue Sky
my auntie Brenda Marshall

To the dead:

Arden Tinmouth — my Uncle Ardie
Pat Lowther
Virginia "Ginny" Louise Tinmuth (Gram)
Paulette Laurendeau
Damon York
Freya Milne
Ramon Hotz

May every poet in the world receive her or his niffler!

Christine Lowther is the author of *My Nature*, *New Power*, and the co-editor/co-author of *Writing the West Coast: In Love with Place*. Her work has appeared in anthologies and periodicals including *The New Quarterly*, *The Fiddlehead*, *British Columbia Almanac*, *The Vancouver Sun*, *Walk Myself Home: An Anthology to End Violence Against Women*, *Risking for Change*, *Salt in Our Blood*, *Crowlogue*, *Wild Moments: Adventures with Animals in the North*, *The Beaver*, and seastories.org. Christine co-teaches writing workshops in Tofino on Vancouver Island, Canada.

Other Books of Interest

Harry Potter

The Order of Harry Potter: The Literary Skill of the Hogwarts Epic
Colin Manlove

Colin Manlove, a popular conference speaker and author of over a dozen books, has earned an international reputation as an expert on fantasy and children's literature. His book, *From Alice to Harry Potter*, is a survey of 400 English fantasy books. In *The Order of Harry Potter*, he compares and contrasts *Harry Potter* with works by "Inklings" writers J.R.R. Tolkien, C.S. Lewis and Charles Williams; he also examines Rowling's treatment of the topic of imagination; her skill in organization and the use of language; and the book's underlying motifs and themes.

The Deathly Hallows Lectures:
The Hogwarts Professor Explains Harry's Final Adventure
John Granger

In *The Deathky Hallows Lectures*, John Granger reveals the finale's brilliant details themes and meanings. Even the most ardent of Harry Potter fans will be surprised by and delighted with Granger's explanation of the three dimensions of meaning in Deathly Hallows. Ms. Rowling has said that alchemy sets the "parameters of magic" in the series after reading the chapter-length explanations of Deathly Hallows as the final stage of the alchemical Great Work, the serious reader will understand how important literary alchemy is in understanding Rowling's artistry and accomplishment.

Repotting Harry Potter: A Professor's Guide for the Serious Re-Reader
Rowling Revisited: Return Trips to Harry, Fantastic Beasts, Quidditch, & Beedle the
Bard
Dr. James W. Thomas

In *Repotting Harry Potter* and his sequel book *Rowling Revisited*, Dr. James W. Thomas points out the humor, puns, foreshadowing and literary parallels in the Potter books. In *Rowling Revisted*, readers will especially find useful three extensive appendixes – "Fantastic Beasts and the Pages Where You'll Find Them," "Quidditch Through the Pages," and "The Books in the Potter Books." Dr. Thomas makes re-reading the Potter books even more rewarding and enjoyable.

Harry Potter & Imagination: The Way Between Two Worlds
Travis Prinzi

Imaginative literature places a reader between two worlds: the story world and the world of daily life, and challenges the reader to imagine and to act for a better world. Starting with discussion of Harry Potter's more important themes, *Harry Potter & Imagination* takes readers on a journey through the transformative power of those themes for both the individual and for culture by placing Rowling's series in its literary, historical, and cultural contexts.

Hog's Head Conversations: Essays on Harry Potter
Travis Prinzi, Editor
Ten fascinating essays on Harry Potter by popular Potter writers and speakers including John Granger, James W. Thomas, Colin Manlove, and Travis Prinzi.

Poets and Poetry

Remembering Roy Campbell: The Memoirs of his Daughters, Anna and Tess
Introduction by Judith Lütge Coullie, Editor
Preface by Joseph Pearce

Anna and Teresa Campbell were the daughters of the handsome young South African poet and writer, Roy Campbell (1901-1957), and his beautiful English wife, Mary Garman. In their frank and moving memoirs, Anna and Tess recall the extraordinary, and often very difficult, lives they shared with their exceptional parents. Over 50 photos, 344 footnotes, timeline of Campbell's life, and complete index.

In the Eye of the Beholder: How to See the World Like a Romantic Poet
Louis Markos

Born out of the French Revolution and its radical faith that a nation could be shaped and altered by the dreams and visions of its people, British Romantic Poetry was founded on a belief that the objects and realities of our world, whether natural or human, are not fixed in stone but can be molded and transformed by the visionary eye of the poet. Unlike many of the books written on Romanticism, which devote many pages to the poets and few pages to their poetry, the focus here is firmly on the poems themselves. The author thereby draws the reader intimately into the life of these poems. A separate bibliographical essay is provided for readers listing accessible biographies of each poet and critical studies of their work.

The Cat on the Catamaran: A Christmas Tale
John Martin

Here is a modern-day parable of a modern-day cat with modern-day attitudes. Riverboat Dan is a "cool" cat on a perpetual vacation from responsibility. He's *The Cat on the Catamaran* – sailing down the river of life. Dan keeps his guilty conscience from interfrering with his fun until he runs into trouble. But will he have the courage to believe that it's never too late to change course? (For ages 10 to adult)

"Cat lovers and poetry lovers alike will enjoy this whimsical story about Riverboat Dan, a philosophical cat in search of meaning."
Regina Doman, author of *Angel in the Water*

Diary of an Old Soul & The White Page Poems
George MacDonald and Betty Aberlin

The first edition of George MacDonald's book of daily poems included a blank page opposite each page of poems. Readers were invited to write their own reflections on the "white page." MacDonald wrote: "Let your white page be ground, my print be seed, growing to golden ears, that faith and hope may feed." Betty Aberlin responded to MacDonald's invitation with daily poems of her own.

Betty Aberlin's close readings of George MacDonald's verses and her thoughtful responses to them speak clearly of her poetic gifts and spiritual intelligence. Luci Shaw, poet

George MacDonald

In the Near Loss of Everything: George MacDonald's Son in America
Dale Wayne Slusser

In the summer of 1887, George MacDonald's son Ronald, newly engaged to artist Louise Blandy, sailed from England to America to teach school. The next summer he returned to England to marry Louise and bring her back to America. On August 27, 1890, Louise died leaving him with an infant daughter. Ronald once described losing a beloved spouse as "the near loss of everything". Dale Wayne Slusser unfolds this poignant story with unpublished letters and photos that give readers a glimpse into the close-knit MacDonald family. Also included is Ronald's essay about his father, *George MacDonald: A Personal Note*, plus a selection from Ronald's 1922 fable, *The Laughing Elf*, about the necessity of both sorrow and joy in life.

Behind the Back of the North Wind:
Critical Essays on George MacDonald's Classic Children's Book
Editors, John Pennington and Roderick McGillis

This collection of 16 essays by various scholars is the first compendium on a particular MacDonald book – *At the Back of the North Wind*. This novel makes a good representative study because it bridges the world of the "realistic" and the fanciful, including a fairy tale and some nonsense poetry. Plus it deals with a central MacDonald theme - death. Essays run the gamut from exploring MacDonald's Christian worldview, to examining the tension between fantasy and reality, to grappling with *North Wind* as children's literature. In every case, the essays illuminate a complex book. This book is also an excellent companion to the critical and scholarly edition of *At The Back of the North Wind* by Pennington and McGillis published by Broadview Press.

A Novel Pulpit: Sermons From George MacDonald's Fiction
David L. Neuhouser

"In MacDonald's novels, the Christian teaching emerges out of the characters and story line, the narrator's comments, and inclusion of sermons given by the fictional preachers. The sermons in the novels are shorter than the ones in collections of MacDonald's sermons and so are perhaps more accessible for some. In any case, they are both stimulating and thought-provoking. This collection of sermons from ten novels serve to bring out the 'freshness and brilliance' of MacDonald's message."

from the author's introduction

George MacDonald: Literary Heritage and Heirs
Roderick McGillis, editor

This latest collection of 14 essays sets a new standard that will influence MacDonald studies for many more years. George MacDonald experts are increasingly evaluating his entire corpus within the nineteenth century context.

This comprehensive collection represents the best of contemporary scholarship on George MacDonald. Rolland Hein, author of *George MacDonald: Victorian Mythmaker.*

C. S. Lewis

C. S. Lewis: Views From Wake Forest - Essays on C. S. Lewis
Michael Travers, editor

Contains sixteen scholarly presentations from the international C. S. Lewis convention in Wake Forest, NC. Walter Hooper shares his important essay "Editing C. S. Lewis," a chronicle of publishing decisions after Lewis' death in 1963.

"Scholars from a variety of disciplines address a wide range of issues. The happy result is a fresh and expansive view of an author who well deserves this kind of thoughtful attention."

Diana Pavlac Glyer, author of *The Company They Keep*

The Hidden Story of Narnia:
A Book-By-Book Guide to Lewis' Spiritual Themes
Will Vaus

A book of insightful commentary equally suited for teens or adults – Will Vaus points out connections between the *Narnia* books and spiritual/biblical themes, as well as between ideas in the *Narnia* books and C. S. Lewis' other books. Learn what Lewis himself said about the overarching and unifying thematic structure of the Narnia books. That is what this book explores; what C. S. Lewis called "the hidden story" of Narnia. Each chapter includes questions for individual use or small group discussion.

C. S. Lewis: His Literary Achievement
Colin Manlove

"This is a positively brilliant book, written with splendor, elegance, profundity and evidencing an enormous amount of learning. This is probably not a book to give a first-time reader of Lewis. But for those who are more broadly read in the Lewis corpus this book is an absolute gold mine of information. The author gives us a magnificent overview of Lewis' many writings, tracing for us thoughts and ideas which recur throughout, and at the same time telling us how each book differs from the others. I think it is not extravagant to call C. S. Lewis: His Literary Achievement a tour de force."

Robert Merchant, *St. Austin Review*, Book Review Editor

C. S. Lewis & Philosophy as a Way of Life: His Philosophical Thoughts
Adam Barkman

C. S. Lewis is rarely thought of as a "philosopher" per se despite having both studied and taught philosophy for several years at Oxford. Lewis's long journey to Christianity was essentially philosophical – passing through seven different stages. This 624 page book is an invaluable reference for C. S. Lewis scholars and fans alike

Why I Believe in Narnia:
33 Reviews and Essays on the Life and Work of C.S. Lewis
James Como

Chapters range from reviews of critical books , documentaries and movies to evaluations of Lewis' books to biographical analysis.
"A valuable , wide-ranging collection of essays by one of the best informed and most accute commentators on Lewis' work and ideas."
Peter Schakel, author of *Imagination & the Arts in C.S. Lewis*

C. S. Lewis Goes to Heaven: A Reader's Guide to The Great Divorce
David G. Clark

This is the first book devoted solely to this often neglected book and the first to reveal several important secrets Lewis concealed within the story. Lewis felt his imaginary trip to Hell and Heaven was far better than his book *The Screwtape Letters*, which has become a classic. Clark has taught courses on Lewis for more than 30 years and is a New Testament and Greek scholar with a Doctor of Philosophy degree in Biblical Studies from the University of Notre Dame. Readers will discover the many literary and biblical influences Lewis utilized in writing his brilliant novel.

Mythopoeic Narnia: Memory, Metaphore, and Metamorphosis
in C. S. Lewis's The Chronicles of Narnia
Salwa Khoddam

Dr. Khoddam offers a fresh approach to the *Narnia* books based on an inquiry into Lewis' readings and use of classical and Christian symbols. She explores the literary and intellectual contexts of these stories, the traditional myths and motifs, and places them in the company of the greatest Christian mythopoeic works of Western Literature. In Lewis' imagination, memory and metaphor interact to advance his purpose – a Christian metamorphosis. *Mythopoeic Narnia* helps to open the door for readers into the magical world of the Western imagination.

Speaking of Jack: A C. S. Lewis Discussion Guide
Will Vaus

Included here are introductions to most of Lewis' books as well as questions designed to stimulate discussion about Lewis' life and work. These materials have been "road-tested" with real groups made up of young and old, some very familiar with Lewis and some newcomers. *Speaking of Jack* may be used in an existing book discussion group or small group, to start a C. S. Lewis Society, or as a guide to your own exploration of Lewis' books.

Pop Culture

To Love Another Person: A Spiritual Journey Through Les Miserables
John Morrison

The powerful story of Jean Valjean's redemption is beloved by readers and theater goers everywhere. In this companion and guide to Victor Hugo's masterpiece, author John Morrison unfolds the spiritual depth and breadth of this classic novel and broadway musical.

Through Common Things: Philosophical Reflections on Popular Culture
Adam Barkman

"Barkman presents us with an amazingly wide-ranging collection of philosophical reflections grounded in the everyday things of popular culture – past and present, eastern and western, factual and fictional. Throughout his encounters with often surprising subject-matter (the value of darkness?), he writes clearly and concisely, moving seamlessly between Aristotle and anime, Lord Buddha and Lord Voldemort. . . . This is an informative and entertaining book to read!"

Doug Blomberg, Professor of Philosophy, Institute for Christian Studies

Spotlight:
A Close-up Look at the Artistry and Meaning of Stephenie Meyer's Twilight Novels
John Granger

Stephenie Meyer's *Twilight* saga has taken the world by storm. But is there more to *Twilight* than a love story for teen girls crossed with a cheesy vampire-werewolf drama? *Spotlight* reveals the literary backdrop, themes, artistry, and meaning of the four Bella Swan adventures. *Spotlight* is is the perfect gift for serious *Twilight* readers.

Virtuous Worlds: The Video Gamer's Guide to Spiritual Truth
John Stanifer

Popular titles like *Halo 3* and *The Legend of Zelda: Twilight Princess* fly off shelves at a mind-blowing rate. John Stanifer, an avid gamer, shows readers specific parallels between Christian faith and the content of their favorite games. Written with wry humor (including a heckler who frequently pokes fun at the author) this book will appeal to gamers and non-gamers alike. Those unfamiliar with video games may be pleasantly surprised to find that many elements in those "virtual worlds" also qualify them as "virtuous worlds."

Fiction

The Iona Conspiracy (from The Remnant Chronicles book series)
Gary Gregg

Readers find themselves on a modern adventure through ancient Celtic myth and legend as thirteen year old Jacob uncovers his destiny within "the remnant" of the Sporrai Order. As the Iona Academy comes under the control of educational reformers and ideological scientists, Jacob finds himself on a dangerous mission to the sacred Scottish island of Iona and discovers how his life is wrapped up with the fate of the long lost cover of *The Book of Kells*. From its connections to Arthurian legend to references to real-life people, places, and historical mysteries, *Iona* is an adventure that speaks to eternal truths as well as the challenges of the modern world. A young adult novel, *Iona* can be enjoyed by the entire family.

CPSIA information can be obtained at www.ICGtesting.com
Printed in the USA
238601LV00003B/1/P